Last Night -

an *Angel* Stopped By . . . .

by

Logan Clarke

and

Darnell Logan-Clarke

and the <u>*angel*</u> who helped us write this . . .

Tearabar, Ltd.
P.O. Box 1894
Lake Arrowhead, CA 92352

Last Night -
an *Angel* Stopped By . . . .

Published by
Tearabar, Ltd.
P.O. Box 1894
Lake Arrowhead, CA 92352
www.tearabar.com

ISBN: 0-9706363-0-X

Library of Congress Catalog Card Number:
Pending

First Printing
Printed in the United States of America

Cover Photo by: Carolyn Q. Phillips
Designed by: Doña Davis-Clarke

I

All I could hear was the whirling sound of the siren and the screeching of the tires. As we careened around every corner, I drifted back to my childhood and remembered that, as a young boy, my dad would often take me for a ride on his beautiful, shiny red fire truck. He'd even let me blow the air horn. We lived in a small town in the '50's and weren't worried about scandals, the insurance risk my dad was taking, or the embarrassment to the fire department if I fell off, and so forth. We lived in relatively peaceful times. Watts/Los Angeles was just another little town on the "other side of the railroad tracks."

When I was growing up, I didn't see much of my dad. Unlike most parents in the early '50's, mine were divorced. Mom was a cabaret and intimate club singer and life was lived out of a suitcase and in the rehearsal hall. My brother and I pitched quarters in the alley behind the clubs. We weren't what you would call a "church-going family" - - my mom never cared much for organized religion. Instead, she taught us we could have a wonderful and true relationship with God regardless of any church or man-made denomination.

"God created Man," she said, "and Man created religion."

My mind came back to the present and I felt something tight. . . constricting my chest. The sirens. . . I knew it was an ambulance. I can tell sirens apart. They all make distinctly different sounds to the trained ear. My dad taught me the difference.

I realized the pressure across my chest came from straps holding me securely to a gurney and that I was inside a speeding ambulance. The next thing I knew, paramedics were wheeling me down a stark, white hallway. All white. . . white walls, white ceilings, sheets, chairs. . . all white. The hallways were deserted. The few people that <u>did</u> come into focus were all wearing white. . . and talking to each other as though I wasn't around. "My God", I thought, "I'm dead. No, I'm in a coma. . . dead people don't have IV's piercing their flesh!" With that thought, I felt instant relief rushing through me. There was still hope.

Immediately, people were sticking needles into the clear tubes hanging from the IV bags and I watched in fascination as the syringes slowly oozed their magic potions. Within seconds, I began to doze.

II

Upon awakening, I realized that I had been moved to another room. I began to see much more clearly and as I took in my new surroundings, I saw an elderly woman with her family in tears gathered around her hospital bed. It wasn't the morgue, but close to it. "Maybe it's the 'pit stop' before you check out," I thought.

Trying to speak was not an easy task. We're talking "cotton mouth," the kind you get from drinking a good slug of milk of magnesia. All I could do was watch as I lay there quietly. The old woman's family seemed to be saying their farewells. . .

their last, as they all kissed and left, handkerchiefs pulled from every person's pocket or purse.

The old woman slowly turned her head in my direction and we locked eyes for a long moment. I couldn't help wondering if she was as confused and frightened as I was. She didn't seem sad, however. There was more a look of acceptance on her face. She seemed to know instinctively that this was her fate and she was tallying up her whole life; where it had brought her and where it was taking her. I wondered if I could have read that much in her face if I hadn't been lying there next to her, unsure of my own fate.

"They call this the Extreme Care Room," she said quietly, her lips carefully enunciating each word. "It's closest to the nurse's station for folks who are just too tired to go on. . . or too hurt to know."

"How long did they say you'd be here?" That was my very feeble way of asking if she was dying.

"Just until the good Lord has time to come for me, son," the woman replied.

"Oh, I'm sorry," I said weakly.

"Why?" she shot back bluntly. "I'm certainly not! I've had a good life. It's time to move on. The people I'm worried about just left here in tears. All <u>they</u> have to look forward to is the grieving process. But me, well. . ."

She paused, smiled and went into that memory bank that I, myself, often slip into.

"I keep hearing my daddy say his favorite line," the old woman said to the ceiling. "'Who knows . . . that life may be death and death be but life itself.' It sure makes a lot more sense, now."

For some reason, I knew the words that were about to come out of my mouth were sincere and I wasn't at all shy asking the old woman, "Does that mean you have had an experience with God, ma'am?"

A genuine and gentle smile came to her lips. "Our whole life is an experience with God, son. We're not abandoned when we're put here. For some people, their entire life on earth is one continuous search for God. For many, the search is never completed until death. But, the lucky ones find God while they're still enjoying life here. Those are the ones who aren't really afraid to die. They may not want to right away, because they have dreams and plans, but we all know our life here is but a brief moment in the overall scheme."

"You sound so sure ma'am. I mean, so matter-of-fact. Have you seen something or been told?"

"The angels tell you."

"Excuse me. . .?"

"The angels. They help to prepare you for the transition."

"Do we <u>all</u> have angels, ma'am?" Deep down inside, I was begging her to say, "yes."

"Of course," she sighed. "Mine is just a little closer right now. She's sort of 'on call.' I imagine she's nearby. It's getting pretty close now."

"If you're completely at peace with dying, does that mean you're at peace with your life here?"

"Yes, both spiritually and emotionally. On my path to heaven, I have found God, peace and truth. There's nothing more that I need."

"You know what I think, ma'am? I think people have a hard time living with the truth or maybe they just don't know it themselves. When I say truth, I don't mean the opposite of lying, but things that are truisms, facts of life and death. And, more importantly, life and the truth in things like love. You know, if we all recognized the truth, it wouldn't be so easy to get sidetracked, especially if we knew the truth about communicating with God. Is it really necessary to read a whole bible to learn how? What if someone can't read? Or can't go to a certain church on a certain day? And do you really need to say a certain prayer or phrase to get God's attention? To be honest, ma'am,

I'm not really big on organized religion and holy roller preachers on TV." I knew I was rambling, but I couldn't help it.

"Good, neither is God, " she shot back with a wink. "I used to love Mark Twain when I was a little girl. Mr. Twain knew the truth. He wrote, 'A real Christian is as cool as a gambler holding four aces.' Now, that's truth. No one needs to be a fanatic, nor do they need to threaten or entice others who don't agree with their brand of religion."

"What about truth in loving or living with your fellow man?" I asked. "What about the truth of justice today? Is it true there's a secret prayer to get into heaven and if you don't say it, or know it, you really go to hell? I know every religion has its answers for all these questions and the Supreme Court is supposedly the ultimate truth in law and justice. But is that true? Or do they even recognize a truism anymore after they have selectively torn each one apart to fit the narrow-minded version their group has?"

I found myself staring at the ceiling as my questions trailed off. The old woman appeared to be dozing, but surprised me with a last comment.

"You sure have a heap full of questions, son. I hope you find your angels early enough in your life to find the answers. And, by the way, you may call me Bettye." With that, she drifted to her own angels or dreams. I looked closely at her respirator and saw she was still alive and just resting. I quietly said a prayer that she would still be there when I awoke.

III

My eyes opened as though my name was being called. It was pitch-black outside the windows and only the small night-lights flickered over each of our beds. You could see the moon reflecting off the lake that our town had been built around. The "cotton mouth" had gone, but the drowsiness was ever-present. Bettye was sitting up in her bed and putting on light makeup while another woman in a pink chiffon dress held a mirror up to Bettye's face. This other woman looked ethereal--with a slight glow around her. As I sat up a little in my bed, the two ladies looked over and smiled, then turned away.

They began talking as the other woman combed Bettye's thick gray hair. It was as though Bettye was intentionally asking the same questions I had just asked of her the previous day.

"You know, Amanda," Bettye began. "Maybe it's the last minute jitters, but there is so much I don't understand about my life. I mean. . . here I am, comfortably accepting my death or 'passing on', as you angels say, and yet I'm not sure I learned what I should have. I found God and peace in my fate but what was it all about? I spent eighty-six years going through all of life's emotions and yet I don't really understand much about why . . . do angels understand that, Amanda?"

"*Of course we do, Bettye. . . talk to me,*" the woman called Amanda answered.

"Don't most people ask you tons of questions at this point?" Bettye asked.

"*Some do,*" Amanda answered. "*I guess it depends on how much they have an understanding of life by the time they pass on. People who are afraid have the most questions. Fear can do such terrible things to a human soul.*"

"What about finding truth?" Bettye asked.

"*That's a very big question, Bettye,*" Amanda responded.

"I always thought I'd found it, but I know there's more to truth than accepting God in your life. The real truth on Earth is pretty difficult to find," Bettye said.

I continued to watch and listen intently. The woman called Amanda was putting a beautiful hair clip in Bettye's hair. I remember seeing an angel carved on its opalescent base.

Suddenly, the door opened and a nurse walked into the room. She looked at us with a puzzled expression on her face, then walked toward Bettye and touched the old woman's covers and checked her three IV's.

"Excuse me, what time are visiting hours over?" I asked. She ignored or didn't hear my question as she reached across Bettye's bed.

"Honey, you must be having some dreams," the nurse stated to Bettye, straightening the rumpled bedcovers. The nurse patted the old woman on the leg and turned to leave. As she shut the door behind her, I slowly turned to look at the two women huddled together, smiling brightly and paying little attention to me in the next bed. Other than an occasional glance or nod, there was no acknowledgment of my presence.

I wasn’t really sure what was happening here, but I was certainly not going to pass it up. I wasn't about to turn on a light or press a "call button." I felt like a kid trying to keep a dream going.

"Is that what you search for. . . truth?" Amanda asked.

"I mean the real kind of truth," Bettye insisted.

"What other kind is there?" Amanda followed.

"Well, you know. Truth in life, facts or truisms that cannot be denied. The truth about our dealings with big issues. Issues like Joy - Dreams - Pain - Loving - finding God, talking to Him." Bettye went on, "Which church really can get you to heaven, or can any? There's just. . . just so much. . ." Bettye said, drifting off.

The mysterious woman reached for Bettye's hand and took it in her own. The scent of lilacs, so faint, but distinguishable, filled the air. Amanda's eyes turned in my direction for just a moment, but their effect was startling. Her eyes were a translucent blue, the color of a misty sky at dawn and filled with knowing. Her long, amber-colored hair fell in gentle curls across her slender shoulders and down to her waist and her olive skin looked ever so soft. Although she was obviously an older woman, there was an ageless beauty that emanated from her very being. I couldn't remember ever feeling so safe.

"The Spaniards have a phrase which goes, 'He who speaks the truth, often talks to himself.' It is a wise old saying," Amanda advised Bettye.

"Is there a reason for everything? Is life pre-ordained?" Bettye asked softly.

"God put you in this place and time for a reason, child, just as I know He brings you home for a reason," Amanda went on. *"I may not know all the why's and wherefore's but I know the Lord wants you. You have taken inventory of your life and you've fulfilled your reason for being here."*

I remembered my wife had put my small travel bag on the stand next to me before she left. It held all my toiletries and such, and, as though I were disarming a bomb, I reached inside for my small dictation tape recorder. I sat it on the edge of the bed and clicked it on. I was thankful it didn't stop her from talking. I didn't want to miss one word she was saying. This was one of those moments that few would believe. I wasn't sure myself exactly what to believe, but I could sort all of that out later.

Amanda took a breath and smiled as she leaned forward. *"To have faith, one must oftentimes believe in the improbable. To have vision, one must see beyond the limits of the human eye.*

To have courage, one must know fear, for, in facing fear, we become brave. To gain wisdom, one must seek knowledge, not only for himself but for Mankind. And, within that knowledge, he shall find truth."

I sat there with my mouth open, hoping the tape recorder was getting every word. "Consider the source," my mother used to say; it was a motto that I tried to live by, as there are endless reams of information that are funneled into our lives on a daily basis. Only by considering the source are we able to separate reality from fantasy, fact from fiction, truth from lies.

It didn't take a genius to know that this was definitely one of those ultimate sources. A divine conversation -- at the very least, an angel or a vision. I preferred to think of her as an angel. I was listening so intently, I could hear the rapid pounding of my own heart when they weren't speaking. Amanda reached over and lightly brushed away the hair that fell across Bettye's forehead, like a mother does to a young child.

"People can't search for truth the same way they search for hidden treasure, perhaps thinking they'll find it like you find a lucky penny. That's not how it works. The truth is very personal. It is not something we can just preach about. No one can be force-fed the truth -- it comes to us one spoonful at a time. It's possible to share the truth with someone, but that doesn't mean he will have faith in that truth in comparison to the one he finds for himself. It comes from within oneself and once recognized and accepted, it will guide and comfort us through that which we call life.

"God is saddened at the droves of his misguided, innocent children who are lured into religious and spiritualistic falsehoods. There are those in this world who preach and yell the

"Gospel", a word which simply means "good news", to the high heavens in the name of the Lord, and they can be <u>*so*</u> *convincing.*

"Unfortunately, many of God's children, who are lost or confused, empty their meager pockets and bank accounts and fill the offering plate. Too often, the money slides from the plate to the pockets of those cowards who hide their greed behind the name of the Lord. If people could just remember that religion was created by man, not God. Many times, organized religion is more about raising funds than raising spiritual awareness.

"Organizing people with the same religious beliefs is wonderful. Churches and hundreds of organizations do so and people do wonderful, charitable work. Oftentimes, they even save a lost soul or two. A large share of the world's population needs that structure and womb-like atmosphere to either share their beliefs or, oftentimes, to strengthen their own faith. There is no wrong in any of that. Unfortunately, most of these

organizations go the path of 'Our way or no way,' and that's when they cross the line. After that, they go on to personalizing religion and faith. That's dangerous.

"There is a universal truth that underlies all religious beliefs, but people somehow encase that truth in shadows of fear, doubt and guilt.

"Most 'churches' depict a room with only three doors: heaven behind door number one, but only if you strictly follow a particular interpretation of the Bible; door number two is purgatory, which by the way, is never mentioned in the Bible -- not once. The Church invented purgatory as a little scare tactic; and the big H is behind door number three.

"These religious groups, organizations or sects take the inner truth in the Bible to some of the most bizarre lengths imaginable. My God. . . thirty-some people commit group

suicide to hitch a ride on a spaceship behind a comet? Give the Lord a break!

"Do you know that in some countries Easter is celebrated by having a man re-enact Jesus carrying his cross to his crucifixion? The finale is actually nailing the man to the cross. I'm talking about real nails through this man's hands and feet! Does anybody really believe God wants to see this kind of religious fanaticism? Heavens no, child. It <u>hurts</u> God to see any of his children suffer. These are very misguided people.

"What you people call 'life' is just a journey in time. We chuckle at those of you who believe your time from birth to death is all there is. There is no human on earth who can truly say, 'This is as good as it gets.' No matter how wonderful and fulfilled his life may be here on earth, it is slight in comparison to the serenity and fulfillment of Heaven.

"Science has known for years that a human utilizes less than ten percent of his brain, even though everyone knows the brain is capable of feats and powers far beyond present day use. So why is it so hard to believe that your journey on earth is less than ten percent of your full journey in life? When you pass on from here, the only thing that dies is your physical participation in the events at this level of life. I passed on from my earthly journey long ago, yet, as you can see, I still have an involvement or an effect on earth. I just don't physically participate." With that, she turned and looked intently at Bettye.

"Is everyone who dies an angel?" Bettye inquired.

"No, no. Just as not everyone on earth is a nurse or a person of the cloth. We all have our purpose," Amanda stated.

"Should everyone's purpose be to help his fellow man, like nurses, priests or angels?" Bettye pressed on.

"*Certainly not,*" Amanda said. "*If it is within your power to help your fellow man, then you should feel obliged to do so. But not because it will help you in your next journey. Do it because you want to, not because you think it will impress God. You can't bargain your way into heaven. Some of the greatest help given to your fellow man is a by-product of someone else being here. There are only a few souls who are destined from birth to devote their entire lives to helping others or in the service of their Lord. Others do it because of a miraculous occurrence in their lives.*"

"Were we all put here for a particular reason?" Bettye asked softly, her voice barely above a whisper.

I couldn't believe it. . . Bettye was asking all the questions I would ask of an angel should I ever have had such a heavenly encounter. It seemed Bettye was there only as a "medium" for my own troubled thoughts as I lay there, uncertain of my own destiny.

" *'A particular reason?' Oh, yes,"* Amanda continued, *"Every life on earth has a definite purpose, but not just to jump in a river and save someone from drowning or to invent a cure for cancer. Those are contributions to your fellow man. Besides, God figures it's up to you to cure cancer, since it's one of the many diseases Man is responsible for. You create pollution -- if you want it fixed, then you fix it. Planting flowers and trees or being there to help someone through a dark period in his life -- all of these are beautiful but they are not preordained reasons for your existence here on earth. Only God has the overall plan and knows why He put you here."*

"If God is there for everyone and knows no prejudice, then why are there so many disasters, diseases, rapes, mutilations, and other human tragedies, like when kids shoot and kill other children?" Bettye asked with concern.

*"God does not preordain that, either. People aren't born bad or evil, they become that way. Why would the Almighty bring such evil upon his own children? Never forget that you were all given **FREE WILL**. What you do in your life is mostly your own doing. Don't get me wrong, there are times when the Lord will step right into your life, either directly or indirectly. Like through an angel. We don't come to you only when it's your time to pass on, for goodness sake. Most times, angels are around to help your life here on Earth. Perhaps you're heading down the wrong path or failing to see what God knows you need to see."*

"Like my heart attack?" Bettye asked.

"The Lord was just reminding you that He was going to be calling you home soon. He is giving you a chance to say goodbye to those you will leave behind. It's not always lightning bolts and visions, though. Your parents and upbringing are greatly responsible for molding much of the life you have on earth. As you grow older, your encounters with your fellow man and your personal victories and defeats within yourself will guide or alter your life greatly, as will your faith in God."

"I've always felt like I could talk directly to God, although He never spoke back to me or anything. . . " Bettye admitted.

"How do you know that?" Amanda questioned.

Bettye paused, "Well, because I never heard Him."

"Maybe not right at that moment, like a conversation with another human, but you hear Him. Believe me, everybody does. If you speak to God, He will always hear you and when He answers you, you will know. Now, whether you choose to 'listen' to Him or not is another matter. That is up to you. If you are doing something that even you know is wrong, God will tell you to do right. If you choose not to, then you reap the consequences. Sometimes, in order to hear something, you must be quiet and take time to have enough faith so that you will recognize His 'voice.' Many times, God's voice is regarded as a conscience speaking. You certainly don't need a large group, stained glass or a million dollar church to speak to God. You have a direct line that is never busy. Use it.

"God put you on this earth and He decides when it is time for you to leave, not you. Those who commit suicide are the most misguided of all. He is here for you, if you wish, but God rarely ***forces*** *His will on your life. Neither does He* ***'punish***

you' in order to get you ***'in line.'*** *He may try to warn you, but He doesn't give ultimatums. Man does that. God never intended for His children to be afraid or to become 'God-fearing people.' God guides with love, never controls with fear. Life is hard enough to get through and understand as it is; why would God want everyone to be afraid of Him? Humans need to have power or control over others -- the Heavenly Father has no such need.*

"If there is a universal truth, then there must be universal laws. . . infinite laws of life, far beyond the laws of a nation. When the infinite laws are broken, your soul must serve time . . . a 'sentence' handed down by you. The hell that goes on inside a tormented soul, who has violated the natural laws of the Universe, is more horrific than any penance God would ever put forth on one of his children. You make your own hell on earth. ***The light is there within us all, waiting only to shine."***

Amanda paused and gently touched the top of Bettye's head. In almost a whisper, she continued, "*There are so many paths that lead to God. The rest of your journey will be a smooth one.*"

"So . . . all beliefs, all people, not just Christians, are God's children? Buddhist, Muslim, Jewish?" Bettye inquired.

"*Of course. Even in remote places like the islands of the Far East, where there are tribes who speak unknown languages and read no printed words and are strangers to the name God - they are all still His children. In their own way of communicating, they speak to Him. They may call Him by a different name, but I assure you . . . their God IS your God. He's everyone's God. And there is only one.*"

Evidently, demi-gods don't make it . . .

"Humans don't have a problem accepting the fact there are many nationalities, languages, and customs. Why is it so hard to believe there are so many different types of beliefs in God? He is spoken to and prayed to in all tongues, in all ways. God is a lot more open-minded than most give Him credit for."

"How do we learn to deal with pain?" Bettye asked. "Not like injuries of the flesh, but soul pain. The pain that comes from losing a loved one or ending a marriage or a relationship with someone who is so much a part of us? Tears are an amazing thing and they don't fall only on the outside," Bettye reminded.

"Quite true. But you know, sometimes it's nice to open up the heart and let a little pain come in. It lets you know you're still alive," Amanda said gently, as she looked down at Bettye.

"Yes," Bettye said, "but it seems that happiness passes by so quickly while sadness remains so long."

"Be careful not to be blinded by sorrow -- don't wear your sorrow like a blanket. When you lose a loved one, you're supposed to feel pain and shed tears. Grief is all part of the healing process. The people left here to mourn are the only ones who anguish. The dearly departed, and you will be one soon, have never been so peaceful and inspired as they are in the next journey."

My mouth was open, but I was ever so careful not to breathe the slightest sound. I glanced down at my recorder and noticed I had plenty of tape left. A smile came over me as I regained my focus on this most fascinating exchange of wisdom -- life's most profound secrets and some of Mankind's biggest untruths I could ever have imagined I'd be privy to.

"Getting past the mourning and tears is very difficult for some. Many times, an angel will be sent to help someone end his

mourning. Sadness should never be allowed to engulf you like a wave," Amanda advised, her voice soft and soothing.

"But what about the pain you suffer because you lost someone and he didn't really go anywhere except away from you?" Bettye explained, "For years I tried to write about dealing with this type of pain. After all, I had two marriages and," Bettye continued, almost blushing, "a few broken hearts in-between. Our emotions seem to be the most difficult aspect of life to deal with and keep in control. Love, joy, dreams, pain and sorrow are all things that make up who we are emotionally . . . within ourselves. Something people rarely see . . . do you sort of understand what I mean?" Bettye almost pleaded. "I thought I had it all figured out and I was content. But I really don't know any details," Bettye went on. "Then, recently, I had a conversation with a middle-aged man who assumed I knew all the answers to life, simply because I was so much older than he was, and all of a sudden . . .," Bettye seemed almost frustrated by her lack of answers.

Amanda looked away and finished Bettye's sentence, *"All of a sudden you had endless questions?"*

Amanda got up and slowly walked about the room. She was in a very reflective mood, almost as though she was remembering a lost love during her own life on earth. As she slowly turned around, she spoke again, gently and knowingly.

"The ability to love so deeply is one of God's greatest gifts. You should never be afraid of loving for fear of loving too greatly. If you hold back to avoid going overboard, you will experience very little in this life. Love, in one form or another, is why you are all here. Why else would any species be so emotionally intricate? So daring . . . and so curious?

"It is through experience in living that wisdom and understanding are nurtured. One cannot simply read about heartache, love, sorrow, and the others, and vicariously have complete knowledge of their force and effect on the human spirit. You will never know the pain of an arrow ripping through your flesh, unless, of course, the target is you! Understanding, peace and contentment are all virtues belonging to those who have borne the risk and burden of <u>*living*</u> *their lessons. They are the brave souls who dared experience the arena of life. Win, lose or draw, they participated . . . not just in love, but in life itself.*

"There is nothing on earth quite like falling in love. The excitement and vast range of emotions that are activated and acted upon are staggering. In the name of love, wars have been fought . . . great art has been both created and destroyed, personal tragedies have been inflicted, as well as overcome, through love. Its potential wrath and power are evident in its close proximity to

hate. Hate is a product born solely of Mankind. God hates no one!"

Amanda returned to Bettye's bedside. "*Although you may yearn for the past, humans cannot rise like the Phoenix from the ashes and return to journeys past. At least not in this life! They must move on and make the present and the future, living proof that they are at peace with their past, their loves, their losses and their hearts. . . only t<u>hen</u> will they journey on to the next plane of their existence. Only t<u>hen</u> will they be allowed to journey with the angels . . ."*

I was sure there were questions I wanted to ask, but I wasn't willing to gamble that a noise or voice might startle this woman or angel or whatever she was and make her disappear. It was an indescribable inner feeling to simply accept and be comfortable with the fact that I was listening to and looking at an angel and that she really <u>could</u> disappear into thin air. I was truly convinced that I was a witness to a miracle. That is saying a lot in itself.

She went on, "*The two most powerful and important moments of your life are birth and death. The in-between times are spent learning about life and God. Not just what they mean to Mankind, but to each individual.*

"*In the end, we find that Man's perception of life and death varies a lot among people. It's how you deal with these profound matters that will determine the direction and smoothness of your path in life. How you deal with your fellow man will affect or be affected by the emotions you are questioning. It would take more than a schoolyard of angels to explain to you the meaning, purpose and effect of it all on each person's life. Only God could do that, but I offer a Haiku of sorts for the curious:*

If you ask me about joy

I'll tell you stories

hours long

If you ask me about dreams

I'll paint you pictures

to fill galleries

If you ask me about pain

I'll write you pages

to fill books

And if you ask me about love

I'll tell you about

Joy

Dreams

Pain

"Many times sadness is a direct result of unfulfilled expectations. People should not expect too much in life or from their relationships with others. No one has been guaranteed anything in life. . . other than God's love and, of course, death."

A deep breath came from Bettye and she and Amanda clutched hands.

"Will you come back here to help someone else, after me?"

"Yes. . . I will. . . I will always be here. Right now, <u>you're</u> *my purpose, but I'll return in one form or another."*

"Who will you be sent to help next time?" Bettye asked weakly; I had to strain to hear her words.

"We never really know, but I have my suspicions." With that, Amanda looked in my direction and smiled. There was a bright aura surrounding her but, unlike the bright light we hear about, this light encompassed the faint colors of a rainbow and was truly multi-colored. She traced Bettye's now-still face with her finger, then floated her hand slowly down the entire length of the old woman's body. Bettye's aura followed beneath the movement of Amanda's hand, like a wave returning to reclaim the shore.

"I'll be back someday," were Amanda's parting words. I watched in disbelief as Bettye's aura dissolved in the glow of the rising sunlight, streaming in through the window, followed closely by Amanda.

I grabbed the tape recorder, clicked it off and held it to my chest. "People will never believe this tape. They'll say I staged it or something."

Stunned, I clearly heard Amanda's voice float upon the air, "*Hopefully, the words are recorded in your heart and you won't need to rely on a machine.* *<u>You</u>* *know the truth, Logan. Write about it, help someone else to find it. Go home with your daughter and your wife. They will be so happy to see you stay home more. Follow your heart, son, and try not to confuse spirituality and religion. God will always be there for all of Mankind as He is needed. Get to know Him. . . understand and trust Him. Believe me. . . He knows you.*"

The room was still and Bettye's body lay silent as the morning crept slowly over the mountain top and cascaded across the lake. I knew inside that her body was simply a shell. . . I, myself, had watched her soul transcend, an experience one could never forget in ten lifetimes.

If I could, I would have pushed the morning away and made it hang in someone else's sky. I wished it could have been dawn for days. Not being an angel, I had to succumb to a few winks of sleep and ponder the reality of the entire evening. Was this some drug-induced state that the hospital had put me in? Certainly, that is what my friends and family would believe.

I couldn't fight the sleep. As crazy as it sounds, I tucked the recorder under my pillow with the wondrous thought that it might all be real. I saved the recording for when I awoke.

I wanted to be fresh and objective. To be honest, in case the tape was blank and it was all in my mind, I wanted to at least go to sleep dreaming it was real and savoring the moment. We sometimes do the silliest things at the most crucial times in our lives.

IV

My eyes popped open and I lay there motionless, staring at the white ceiling and the television sticking out of the wall. My eyes rolled toward Bettye's bed and, as I predicted, it was empty. The mattress was stripped, rolled up and bound, the standard procedure at most hospitals when someone dies.

The entire scenario of the previous night replayed itself in my head, right up to putting the tape recorder under my pillow. Anxiously, I slid my hand between the pillow and the still-starched white sheet -- as though I hadn't expected the recording to really be there -- my God, what if it was gone?! -- and retrieved the machine.

Slowly I turned toward the window that overlooks the lake. I eased the recorder to my face and pressed the rewind button. The whirling sound of the recorder faded out. My thoughts and prayers that the recording was real and that I would hear the conversation were overwhelming. Even if I could just prove it to myself, that would be okay.

The click of the tape stopping seemed louder than an engine freezing up at 40 mph. My thumb instantly pressed "play." A long . . . long . . . pause. I listened so intently I clearly heard my heartbeat through the silence on the recorder. My breathing got heavier. My heart rate increased; the silence continued. My mind wandered off, for what was an indeterminable length of time; mustering up prayers for Amanda's voice and curses for the lack of it. Anxiety grew when, suddenly, a voice clearly spoke out from the recorder.

It was Bettye's voice. I turned the volume up slightly and tilted my head, bringing my ear closer to the tiny speaker. I acted as though someone other than myself was going to overhear. "Is everyone who dies an angel?"

My God!! My heart pounded faster. The tape was silent for quite awhile, no sound other than the steady hum of my recorder until Bettye's voice once again boomed out as I cranked up the volume.

"Should everyone's purpose be to help his fellow man, like nurses, priests or angels?"

More silence. My face flushed and my heart seemed to stammer and race alternately. "What was going on?" I asked myself, repeatedly. "How in the world . . .? Why wasn't Amanda's voice there?! Who was Bettye talking to?! For God's sake, what's going on?!"

I quickly hit "fast forward" and then stopped to listen. Silence, then. . .

"I've always felt like I could talk directly to God, although He never spoke back to me or anything . . ."

I slammed the "stop" button and twisted quickly toward the old woman's bed. I clutched the recorder to my chest as I glared at the stripped bed with despair. I must have been dreaming the whole thing. "No, wait . . . if it was my dream, where did Bettye's voice come from? And if Bettye's voice was there. . . where's the voice of her friend Amanda or whoever she was? She was here and had been talking to Bettye!"

"Oh, God," I whispered. I had never known such utter devastation and disappointment. It was so real! Tape recorder and all!! "Could it have been some drug they poured into me? That still didn't explain Bettye asking someone questions. Who was she asking. . . me?"

I fell back against my pillows, still clutching the recorder. I pressed the reclining button to flatten my bed and stared blankly at the ceiling and a smoke alarm with a small red light blinking every 15 seconds to assure its battery was working.

Slowly, the sockets of my eyes filled as a warm, solitary tear rolled down my face. I couldn't think or speak. All the beliefs I had developed over the years . . . my writings, my future. . . were all brought to a reality in a "sign" that I'd been on the right track. And just as quickly they were shaken and ripped to near- destruction.

Then, "Mr. Optimistic" popped into my head for a cheer rally. "Could Amanda have been Bettye's 'angel' come to guide her to the other side? That would explain it. What if you can't record angel voices? That's it! Just like you can't take their picture. Yeah! That's gotta be it! I'm not smart enough to dream all that. Just like she said, "To have faith, one must oftentimes believe in the improbable. To have vision, one must see beyond the limits of the human eye. To have courage, one must know fear, for, in facing fear, we become brave. To gain wisdom, one must seek knowledge, not only for himself but, for Mankind. And, within that knowledge, he shall find truth.' Damn, how did I remember that?"

I vividly flashed on the motion picture, "Miracle on 34th Street," and Edmund Gwenn telling Natalie Wood, "Faith is believing in something when common sense tells you not to." I wanted so desperately to hang onto this miracle, this visit or whatever it was. I had to assure myself that I wasn't conning myself into believing this. Anyone can say he believes he met an angel, and maybe he did, but angels don't leave much behind after they've gone.

"Maybe," I thought. . . "maybe it was just my subconscious talking to me, encouraging me to get back to my writing." I mentally skimmed through the warehouse of literary material stored in my closet. I recited a line from memory:

"Hold dearly to your dreams, for within their reality lies Man's greatest hope!"

I had believed and written that years ago. Maybe just for this moment. And it helped. But I was still severely disappointed. Oh, I'd get over it, but I'd have to pump myself up and keep convincing myself it was real. I knew deep down, each night, as I went to bed, I would wonder and ask myself for the rest of my life: "*Who* was that. . . *what* was that?"

Again, my own writings came to mind:

"In order to have a pocketful of dreams, one must first have a hand filled with vision."

"So what if it was just a dream?" That familiar little voice inside me said, "Maybe it was meant to be. Go with it," I demanded of myself. I was bound and determined to hold dearly to this moment.

Quite a few years ago, when I first realized that I had found God and was in a process of defining Him to myself, I wrote a poem that I've always liked. It seemed to belong to this moment. I closed my eyes --

I hold dearly to my dreams
They are all alone powerful
and enable me to look beyond -
the bad times.

I hold dearly to my memories
They are my constant reminder
That I have known love, peace and warmth
in an oftentimes -
cruel world.

I hold dearly to my friends
For they are my strength
and help me to continue on
even when I think -
I've given up.

Now,
I have found a common link
Between my friends, dreams and memories
And I hold dearly -
to you.

V

My mind searched endlessly for justification, self-proof and logic to bolster my belief (desire) that it was all real -- that I really <u>had</u> seen an angel and <u>had</u> heard her talking with Bettye. I even recited perfectly a passage of the angel's philosophy. It was all I had to hang on to . . . not much . . . but maybe just enough to get me back to completing the book that had been four years awaiting my return. The book's title, "Until I Journey with the Angels," seemed more than apt. It became a "sign" to myself, more than just mere coincidence.

None of that was tangible proof of my encounter, but it would have to do. I needed to convince myself.

A quick knock on the door of my hospital room and in walked the two loves of my life. My wife Doña and my nine-year-old daughter Darnell. Beaming with smiles and kisses, they told me I was checked-out and ready to go.

While the girls helped me dress and pack my things, Doña noticed the stripped bed beside us. Darnell, of course, picked up on Doña's expression.

"What happened to the lady last night, Papa?" Darnell asked.

"Oh, she passed on early this morning, but she was in no pain. She even had a smile on her face," I quickly responded.

"Maybe she was seeing family members who had died before and she was happy," Darnell added, smiling.

"I think you're right, honey," I replied, as I gazed at my insightful daughter. "I really do."

I left it at that. I knew we would discuss my experience later. We are a very open family and share most everything with each other. The voice on the tape will be most intriguing to them. If it was a dream, whose dream was it? Regardless, I wasn't about to try to recount it right then. I wanted to put the entire incident "on hold." Of course, things don't always go the way we plan.

As we were leaving and Darnell was pushing me in the wheelchair, she decided to use the restroom. Doña said we would wait for her in the hallway and while my wife spoke to my nurse, Nicole, I rolled myself down the brightly lit corridor to gaze into the other rooms. Several patients were quite old and obviously very ill. I wanted so badly to go in and ask them if they had met their angel yet. Fortunately, logic took control and kept me from ending up in a padded room!

I realized Darnell had been gone quite a while and gestured for Doña to check on her. Just as she reached the door, Darnell came walking out carrying a book in her hand. As she began to speak with her mother, her head turned, as though in slow-motion, her long brown hair twirling out behind her. I watched as her small hand reached up to touch a clip in her hair. As she toyed with the clip, I motioned for her to come over to where I sat in the wheelchair. With a big smile, she handed her mother the book, as Doña continued her conversation and exchange of hospital papers with Nicole.

As Darnell approached my wheelchair, I couldn't keep my eyes off the hair clip. I reached up tentatively to touch it.

There was an angel on the clip and it appeared to be carved from mother-of-pearl; her hair was long and curly, just like Amanda's; her dress was even a pinkish color. Slowly, I removed the clip from Darnell's hair.

"Honey, where did you get this?" I asked anxiously, trying to keep my voice steady so I didn't frighten my young daughter.

"A nice lady in the bathroom gave it to me, Papa. She also gave me a book," she answered shyly. "I know I'm not supposed to take presents from strangers, but she was <u>so sweet</u> and somehow I knew I was really safe. Honest, Papa, she even knew my name!"

"Honey, this clip belonged to that lady in my room who passed away this morning. I don't know who gave it to you;

maybe the nurse thought it was yours," I said with some hesitation.

"No, Papa . . . this was not a nurse," Darnell explained. "She even told me to share the book with my family. Honest, Papa, she really wanted me to have it. She said you would understand."

I didn't want to disappoint her, but there was no question that this was the hair clip I had seen the woman in the chiffon dress place in Bettye's lovely, thick gray hair last night. I saw Nicole and called her over. I told her someone had made a mistake. I explained that the hair clip belonged to Bettye and perhaps her family would want to keep it. Her response almost knocked me out of the wheelchair.

"That's very nice of you, Mr. Clarke, but Bettye had been undergoing treatment for brain cancer for many months and she had no hair. In fact, when she first came to us, she was completely bald and never even wore a wig. So, thank you for your honesty, but it didn't belong to Bettye. I'm sorry," Nicole said, "I'm going off duty now, but if you would like to leave the clip at Lost and Found, the other nurse at the desk can show you where it is."

Dumbfounded, I watched her walk away. As I rubbed the angel hair clip, I saw Nicole pull off her nurse's cap, releasing a full head of thick, beautiful, amber hair--just like Amanda's.

My entire body tingled, as though I had been shot up with Novocain and it was starting to wear off. My face felt flushed and my heart was banging so hard I feared my chest would explode from the sheer force of it all.

"I told you, Papa. Can I have it back now?" Darnell's little voice shook me out of my trance.

I mumbled something unintelligible and handed her the clip. I honestly didn't know whether to be elated or spooked. I had never known such confusion.

Doña had finished with the paperwork and now came to walk beside me as Darnell turned and began to push my wheelchair toward the door. None of us said a word on our way to the car.

Doña slipped behind the wheel and, as a light snow began to fall, she carefully drove the two miles of curving highway to our mountain home. The conversation was mainly about the medication and rehab instructions the doctor had left for me.

At home, the girls had already stacked pillows on the couch in anticipation of my arrival. Doña encouraged me to lie back and keep my shattered leg elevated and to cover myself with a large, soft quilt. Our living room was illuminated solely by the crackling flames in the fireplace as, outside, the snow continued to fall and, leaning back against the cushions, I was engulfed in a feeling of peace and well-being . . . home had never felt so good.

Darnell had placed the book she had been given, by the stranger at the hospital, on the coffee table, and I reached over and picked it up. The cover was softly padded with a gauze-like material, the likes of which I had never seen.

The light from the fire cast dancing shadows across the walls and, although the room was dimly lit, the book itself seemed to glow with a light of its own. Like the angel clip, the cover of the book seemed almost incandescent . . . ethereal. Perhaps it was the lingering traces of my medication; or, perhaps the firelight was playing tricks with my eyes -- but I could have sworn that there were angels dancing across the front cover.

"Hey, girls," I began, "Just stop what you're doing for a moment, put the phone on voice mail and come in here and sit down. I've got one incredible story or, should I say, one incredible experience to share with you."

As they settled on the two overstuffed chairs near the fire, Doña said, "We're all ears, honey."

With the book resting on my lap, I carefully began to turn some of the pages, eager to see what they might reveal. They were blank. Confused, I quickly began to flip through all the pages and although they were lined . . . there were no words. None. Only the first page had been written on and the words, in beautiful old English script, seemed to leap off the page:

Your future is in the unwritten words on these pages. Pick up the pen and accept responsibility of being the author.

VI
The Beginning